My life in so many pieces

by

Peter Savill

Memories, mis-memories, contradictions, assumptions and secrets

Copyright © 2024 Peter Savill

ISBN: 978-1-917129-37-4

All rights reserved, including the right to reproduce this book, or portions thereof in any form. No part of this text may be reproduced, transmitted, downloaded, decompiled, reverse engineered, or stored, in any form or introduced into any information storage and retrieval system, in any form or by any means, whether electronic or mechanical without the express written permission of the author.

1

So, it's an itchy hot summer day. The first time I get to see a kingfisher, in the actual feathers as it were. But that's not the reason I remember that July afternoon.

We're walking along the canal towpath, down the line of locks where the Shropshire Plain descends to meet the more commonly known Cheshire one. The series of fourteen locks, the one thing the water-bound holidaymakers always remember about this place, the village where I grew up.

My brother suddenly calls out, far too loudly in the circumstances, 'Over there. Quick!'

It's hard to see anything. The cow parsley is nearly as high as the hawthorn and the blasted sun is streaming through the gaps in the hedge, right in my eyes.

He points. 'There!'

In the louvred slats of light streaming through the hedgerow on the opposite bank, there's a flurry of blue and gold.

'A kingfisher,' my brother announces matter-of-factly, as if an everyday sight. For him maybe. It's taken me 50-odd years to see my first glimpse of the blue and gold of what-might-have-been-a-kingfisher, so I'm glad to take his word for it.

When we were kids, that was the one everyone wanted to see. The kingfisher; king of birds. At least, in terms of rarity and the number of points it merited in your I Spy Out in the Countryside book, or whatever that well-thumbed paperback was called. What I wouldn't have given back in the day to cross that one off. A kingfisher!

We walk on past woods which had been the setting for many childhood battles with cowboys, Indians, or Zulu warriors, not to mention the odd monster and mutant. On past the secret dip, hidden amongst the gorse bushes, where once we'd set up camp for a night under the stars. It was just the once and I'd been safely back home well before midnight.

The next lock holds special memories. Here, boys braver than me, dared to jump over the narrow passageway between the lock gates. Looking over the edge, it's doesn't seem nearly as far down to the muddy water below. The "jump of death" not nearly so life threatening now.

There's the noise of a tractor in the field behind the hedge, accompanied by an overpowering whiff of diesel fumes.

'Alright,' my brother calls out.

'Alright,' a voice replies through the thicket.

My brother smiles smugly as we walk on. 'You know who that was, don't you?' he says.

All I'd seen was a dirty plume of smoke, rising over the top of the hedge.

A pause. 'That's your half-brother.'

What! I'm not sure if he's joking or not. It must be a wind-up. This is my brother, Paul, we're talking about, after all.

'I've got a half-brother?'

'No.' His smugness intensifies. 'Actually, you've got two.'

2

So, I'm being dragged along this narrow country lane by my mother.

Suddenly, she starts to increase her already frantic pace as we approach the spot where the mud-covered farm dogs usually lie in wait, ready to spring and bark, jumping up and rattling the insecure wooden gates as we pass. It's quiet today. That's probably what scares my mother the most, the fact she never knows whether they'll be there or not.

On we go, past the mysterious Bridge House, partly shielded by a line of oak trees on the right. My mother waves, as she always does, but there's no acknowledgement from her reclusive cousins inside.

As we cross over the canal bridge there's an ominous noise overhead, loud enough to make the hedges tremble, loud enough to stop my mother in her tracks.

She pulls me closer towards the protective brambles which arch above us, encasing half the lane in a see-through cover. 'Don't look up and let them see you,' she whispers, even though the noise is deafening.

Too late, I'm already looking. The thunder of engines passing overhead is a common occurrence. The German Heinkel bombers hug the contours of the ground, as much as they dare, to avoid the radar from the nearby R.A.F. station at Tern Hill, flying so low you can see the two pilots sitting in the long greenhouse-like canopy of the cockpit.

Staring up, I fancy I lock eyes with one of the pilots, the suggestion of a smile on his face. Not that he'd be interested in my mother and me. Far bigger fish for him to fry, as he heads on to drop his deadly cargo over Liverpool.

We emerge from the brambles, my mother pulling me as I drag my heels, still watching the plane, moving so slowly away that it looks almost frozen up there in the sky.

This is not actually my story to tell. It belongs to the memories of my eldest brother, David. It might be his story, but I imagine myself there, in his place, an acquired memory that has become every bit as real to me as to him, fresh details presenting themselves with each recollection.

David is the older of my two brothers, considerably older. Annoyingly, he doesn't look it. Not so long ago, a woman in the village ice cream shop mistook me for him, despite him being nineteen years older!

He told me the Heinkel aircraft story readily enough, albeit he'd never spoken about the 'extended' branch of our family before. Both David and Paul, for some reason, have always felt the need to shield their youngest brother from the family secrets.

It was a well-worn path at that time for my mother and David, along the winding country lanes leading down to Cox Bank, to visit her friend, Elsie, whose husband was away fighting in the war.

Only later did my brother discover that it was also a well-worn path for someone else – my father.

3

So, it's his last delivery of the day. A concealed turning leading down the narrow Sandy Lane to the smallholding, half a mile along.

The groceries in the wicker basket on the front of his bicycle rattle, as he negotiates the potholes in the sunken roadway running between the fields, high up on either side. He stops a little way along and rests his foot on a step up to a stile. Through the wooden bars, St James's church and the rest of the village are visible down below, spread out at the foot of Holmes Bank.

Feeling under each armpit in turn, he sniffs, then spits into his hands and smooths down his jet-black hair, ready now to go on to the red bricked farmhouse ahead. He props his bike against the milk-churn stand alongside the entrance to the driveway, smiling and pretending not to notice someone moving quickly out of sight. His arrival has been noticed, for sure.

She's caught his eye before, often in her nurse's uniform, looking from an upstairs window or standing in the gateway, peering down the road as he approached with his deliveries. He'd seen her in the village on her bicycle, spotted her looking in through the shop window a few times, but she'd never come in.

It helped brighten his day. There wasn't much else that did at the moment. Life had been largely uneventful since he'd moved here with his mother to run the grocery shop on the edge of the village, where the road snaked down past the church. His mother had sold a similar shop in Crewe to move here. He wasn't sure why? There hadn't been doorstep deliveries back in West Street and certainly not as many hills to cycle up as there were around here.

He places the groceries on the doorstep before turning back to his bike. Instead of cycling off, he wheels it a short way down the lane and waits in the middle of the roadway.

A moment later she appears out of the driveway on her bike. She's wearing her uniform and has her ginger hair pinned back. As she sees him, she brakes sharply, using her feet as much as her brakes to slither to a stop, just in front of him.

'Hey, steady on,' he laughs, 'or I WILL be needing a nurse.'

She smiles then and nervously turns away as they make eye contact.

'Fred.'

'Joyce.'

'I've seen you around the village.'

'I've seen you in the shop.'

'Bye then.'

'Bye.'

The next week he can see her in the driveway as he cycles along the lane with his delivery. 'Not going to run into me today then,' he says with a smile as he pulls up in front of her.

'Sorry?' Then she remembers. 'Oh, no.'

He starts to move away and then turns. 'There's a dance on in the Public Hall on Saturday,' he says casually.

'Yes, I, er, saw the poster.'

'I was thinking of going.'

A hand rises to pat her hair as she flushes a little. 'Well, I don't know if I will. I might be working this weekend.'

He knows she works at the Sanatorium, six or seven miles away at Loggerheads, just over the Staffordshire border, high up in the hills, to reap the benefit of the wholesome fresh air for its patients recovering from TB and pneumonia. Great for them, but not so good if you had to cycle up there.

He starts to get on his bike. 'Maybe I'll see you there some other time then.'

'*Unless...*' *she blurts out,* 'I might be getting my weekends mixed up.'

He smiles. 'Might see you Saturday then.'

And he did. And that was how my Mum and Dad met.

He was 26 and she 21 when they married at the Methodist Chapel in the village not so very long after that first meeting.

In the kitchen, when I was growing up, there was a sepia picture of them posing with a pretty house in the background. Originally, I had wondered where it was and what the connection was to them, but subsequently found out it was just somewhere couples had their pictures taken at the time, a pretty backdrop for their wedding photographs, up an alleyway from the chapel.

Even as a child it looked old fashioned to me. But there was no denying they made a handsome couple. Dad so smart in his suit and buttonhole. Mum suitably demure, in her long white dress and lacey veil, her arm draped through his and smiling as though she hadn't a care in the world.

4

So, he waits until it's dark. His precious bundle tightly pressed to his chest and wrapped in a fluffy pink woollen blanket, warmed in readiness on the back of a chair in front of the kitchen range. His wife is in the bedroom above, still crying.

He sets off on his bike, gritting his teeth and nodding to himself as he peddles along, as if unconsciously counting, so he won't have to think.

Even though it's late, he avoids the main road through the village and instead pushes his bike along a couple of narrow footpaths skirting the village centre. He passes the pretty house where they had posed for their wedding pictures, on that day which suddenly seems a world away from the circumstances which bring him here now. His destination lies just ahead.

Only when he is sure the main road is empty, does he emerge from the path, cross the carriageway and stand before the cemetery gates.

He leaves his bike behind the wall and walks along the gravel between the elm trees towards the cemetery lodge, trying to avoid crunching the stones beneath his boots as he goes.

There's a flickering light on in the front of the lodge, which surprises him. A figure appears in the doorway as he passes. They see the blanket and nod, pointing to the path leading along the boundary hedge towards the back of the cemetery.

He walks on down the sloping ground, passing a mound of recently disturbed soil. There's a spade next to it. He picks it up and turns back towards the figure from the lodge, who has followed to the top of the pathway. They exchange nods.

Laying the pink blanket delicately down on the ground, he starts to dig.

It wasn't such a bad spot. In daylight, you could see down over the fields to the canal and, across to the right, the black and white timbers of Moss Hall, in the distance the outline of the Bickerton Hills.

Not such a bad spot for an unmarked grave for my prematurely born second brother, John, who not even David got to meet.

5

So, I'm in my pram being pushed along by my sister-in-law, Joy. My mother has run to the gate as we set off. She catches us up and fusses with the blanket covering me. 'Don't forget to keep the sunshade up, will you?' she says. 'It looks like it might be hot.'

Joy smiles and waves as we set off down the lane. Once around the corner, the sunshade is quickly lowered, and she jiggles the handle of the pram. 'Where shall we go today then?'

A sense of ill-ease wells within me, even though I can't see where we're heading. It's as if all outings will end in the same place.

'Who wants to go down the Big Bank?'

My worst fear confirmed. 'No, no, not the Big Bonk,' I plead.

'Don't be silly. It'll be fun,' she says with a smile.

Excuse me, but I happen to know differently. Didn't she once let go of the handle of the pram as we descended the Big Bonk, as I called it? Only as it started to gain momentum, did she catch hold of the handle again.

And this was, after all, the person who was later to teach me the "Peter Martin" mantra, which I recited merrily as a toddler, much to the horror of my mother.

"Peter Martin, fell down farting,
Got up winking, started stinking."

Martin! Still, things could have been worse. Much, much worse.

My mother was convinced a family fortune was waiting to be claimed from "the Goddard face-powder people" as she called them. Not that she knew any of them or anything about them, come to that.

The only connection seemed to be that my father, and his before him, had been given Goddard as a middle name, as if that established some sort of claim to any inheritance money that might be going begging. Well, it did in my mother's eyes.

There was talk of me, apparently, also acquiring the moniker. All things considered, I'm quite happy with Martin.

Surely, I would have been too young to remember? Or is it just something I've been told? Either way, I can picture young Peter Martin being pushed along in his pram towards the end of the world as he knew it, the point where the road dropped out of sight - the Big Bank. Only the promise afterwards of his favourite "red raspberry jelly" to pacify him and then perhaps a bedtime story.

'No, no, not the woof,' I would plead. Guess which one I usually got? Yep, the woof as I used to call it - Little Red Riding Hood.

Seems inevitable that the Big Bank should start its descent at the canal bridge. Bridge House seems to be figuring more prominently in my past than expected.

My first paper round started there. It had money collecting responsibilities attached and earned me the princely sum of one pound ten shillings for just two mornings work. Riches, at least to a 14-year-old in the 1960's! Half a crown a week pocket money had been my only previous source of income and that stopped promptly once my paper round began.

How my employer ever managed a face-to-face with the inhabitants of Bridge House to obtain permission, I don't know? But he must have, for there, inside the tiled open porchway, my pile of papers would be waiting for me every Saturday and Sunday morning, the names of the customers initially pencilled in the top right-hand corners until I knew by heart who had what.

'Whatever you do, don't leave a News of the World where there should be a Sunday Telegraph, or I'll never hear the end of it.'

There wasn't a delivery for Bridge House. They didn't do newspapers.

Bridge House had belonged to my grandfather who sold it to the Edwards family when he retired. They were cousins on my grandmother's side. There was a brother, George, who would sometimes wave to me from the yard, and his sisters. I don't remember seeing anything of them properly, other than their shadowy outlines moving behind the curtains.

There were a few acres of land as well as the house and a range of outbuildings that included stables, where the bargees, as David called them, used to tether their horses for the night.

The inhabitants of Bridge House had not always been so solitary. David recalls visiting there once with his mother and having a cup of tea in the dark sitting room with aspidistras, chenille tablecloth and thick curtains.

Quiet. He remembers it being very quiet. An echo perhaps of the tragedy that was to befall Bridge House years later.

6

So, pushing through the people gathered in the back yard, I run into the garden, frantically looking around. There aren't any flowers readily at hand to pick, but I know where there will be some.

With a little trepidation, I head towards the chicken run, where the fiery combed cockerel, fiercely guards his territory. Whenever there is occasion to venture inside the run to collect eggs, I take something with me to throw to try and distract him. But he knows I'm there to steal from him.

There's no sign of him now. He must be inside the shed. I open the gate as quietly as possible, leaving it ajar behind me, ready for a quick escape.

In the well scratched enclosure, dandelions grow on the few clumps of remaining turf, like palm trees on a litter of islands, scattered in an ocean of soil. The ones nearest the gate will do, even though there are better ones further down inside the pen. I'm not that brave!

Almost at once there's the sound of ruffling feathers, followed by a screech. Snatching up the dandelions, I run for the gate, but the cockerel launches himself at me and a claw snags in the back of my knee length sock. Kicking out wildly I manage to dislodge him. Thankfully, I'm out of the gate before he gets a proper hold of me again.

Putting the peg back over the latch, I breathe out heavily. We stand and survey each other silently for a moment, the cockerel and me, as if neither wants to be the first to look away.

Back in the yard, my mother is crying, my father at her side. I weave through a forest of legs to get to the tiny coffin which rests on one of the kitchen chairs. It is not much *longer than the seat it rests on. Almost immediately it is carried away, with my dandelions laid on the top.*

I had seen Philip briefly from the bedroom doorway, stared as my mother cradled him. Only the top of his head had been visible over the blanket wrapped around him.

A man, my father called Doctor, was standing at the bedroom window with a bent finger to his lips, his battered leather bag at his feet. I was led out and the bedroom door closed behind me. A few moments later the baby's crying stopped, as my mother's reached new heights.

There had been another man before him, who my father called Vicar. He had mumbled something and gesticulated with his arms over the baby as my mother held it, whilst me and Dad stood watching from the doorway.

Another acquired memory courtesy of David that seems so real to me. A second parish grave, but at least this time there is a coffin for little Philip, who had Spina Bifida and died at the age of just two months.

7

So, he leaned back against the lorry cab and took a whiff of his Woodbine, exhaling through his nostrils and breathing the smoke in again.

After their marriage, Joyce's father had provided the funds for him to set up in business and so, for better or worse, he had become a coal merchant, with all that entailed; namely a coal yard, large metal shed and lorry, as well as lungs full of coal dust. These days seemed to be more worse than better.

Today, for example, had been a day and a half. Heavy snow had fallen overnight and drifted in waves, up over the sides of the hedges, creating an artic landscape in the morning sun.

If it hadn't been for his neighbours helping to clear the snow the half mile or so down to the main road, he wouldn't have been able to get to Silverdale Colliery to collect his coal. No doubt they would be reminding him of that when they wanted extra rations.

Cigarette finished, he stubbed the butt under his steel capped boot and took off his well-worn-leather jacket that he wore to load and unload the sacks of coal onto his lorry. As he gave it a shake, he caught his hand on one of the protective metal studs on the back.

'Damn bloody thing,' he shouted at it, as he sucked a bleeding knuckle. Then, after a final dust-down, which served to cover him in a fresh coating of coal dust, he hung the jacket on one of the lorry's wing mirrors. With a final sigh he set off home.

In those days they lived at Newholme, the newly built semi-detached house Mum and Dad rented and had even been allowed to name. Paul and I were both born there. My parents had moved to Newholme when David was a young boy. He promptly developed pneumonia due to the damp, newly plastered walls.

The actual address was Kettle Lane, but my mother never called it that.

In the 1960's the local council erected Kettle Lane signs at the top and bottom of the road. Mum was outraged. Well, she would have been if she could ever have displayed such an emotion.

It was always Kinsey Heath to her. Not Kynsal Heath either, as some people called it. Joy used to tease her and delighted in making sure any letters she sent were addressed to the official postal address!

Not long after the war ended, the coal business was sold to Bob Cliffe, who soon had two galvanised shelters and lorries. Dad went to work at a local company, Bonells. He was known there by his colleagues as FRS, his initials. Goddard was not included or, more likely, known about.

His occupation on my birth certificate is given as "tractor driver", but I always tell people he worked for a firm of agricultural engineers. They did contract work for farmers, and he used to drive one of those great big combine harvesters, the ones motorists love to complain about when they get stuck behind.

Occasionally, he would bring home hares, which had been killed accidentally by his harvester. We, meaning Paul, would take them up the lane to Gertie Whalley for skinning. It didn't take her five minutes to get the job done as she sat outside her back door, bucket at her feet, resplendent in head scarf, rollers, wraparound apron, men's socks and shoes with inch high heels.

Just before I was due to leave secondary school, my Dad told me about a job in the office at Bonells. 'Be good for you,' he said.

That was the first of many battles with my father. At the age of sixteen, he thought I had been "kept long enough" and ought to be contributing to the family income.

By this time, I had decided, rather grandly most people seemed to think, that journalism was for me. This was a bit different from my first career choice, made when I was nine.

We had to write an essay at school entitled 'What I want to do when I leave school'. For me it was obvious. 'I want to be a porter at Crewe Memorial Hospital,' I wrote. A choice, no doubt, influenced by the times in my infancy, spent visiting my mother at various hospitals around Staffordshire and Cheshire.

Even at the age of nine, I had thought it might be too difficult to become a doctor and, anyway, if you were a porter, you could ride around on the back of the trolleys and beds as they were pushed from ward to ward along those endless shiny floored corridors.

One of the earliest memories of my Mum is going to visit her in hospital, being held up so I could see her at the window, waving from her bed. My first alcoholic drink, on my 18th birthday, was on the way back from visiting her at the City General Hospital in Stoke. The Falcon in Woore. A gin and orange.

My mum's health deteriorated soon after I was born. Though never said, I always felt it implied that it was somehow my fault. She had asthma.

After a hospital porter, it was a journalist. I wasn't quite sure why, not knowing exactly what working on a newspaper entailed. Writing was my love and so I assumed that would be the right option.

A career as a journalist wasn't seen as realistic for a secondary modern school pupil. At a school careers convention when journalism was mentioned, they pointed me towards the far corner and the hand-written sign declaring, "Other Occupations". Not that anyone knew anything about it there either. If Mum had gone with me she would have steered me towards banking or something deemed more suitable. Dad didn't see any point in Career Conventions, as long as you were earning.

My commerce teacher raised her hands in horror when she heard what I wanted to do. 'You mean you want to go and work on the Chronicle?' she gasped.

Anyway, my mind was made up. I read some books in the library and enrolled on the commercial course in the third year at Shavington Secondary Modern to learn shorthand and typing. Not many boys took that course, I can tell you, and it led to a bit of heckling.

Mrs Dodd, our typing instructor, used to have this old wind-up gramophone which played scratchy staccato music to encourage even typing. She would prowl up and down the classroom to make sure no-one was looking at their fingers.

"Carriage return. Fingers on the home keys," she would shout as a cacophony of typewriter bells rang out on various Imperial and Remington machines at the end of each typed line.

Halfway through my A levels at Dane Bank College there was renewed pressure from Dad for me to contribute to the family finances, so I started looking for work. And it was thanks to my shorthand and typing qualifications that I managed to get a job on a local paper. It wasn't the Chronicle, but it was a job on a newspaper.

I'll be forever grateful to one of my old classmates, Hazel Challinor, who handed me a copy of the Newport and Market Drayton Advertiser when I was delivering my papers one Saturday morning. It was open at the page with an advert for a trainee reporter. Never did thank her properly.

Everyone seemed surprised when I got the job, except for me. You do have unshakeable faith in yourself at that age, don't you?

My Dad was happy I would be earning seven pounds a week. 'Good money for someone your age.' Not that I saw much of it. Three pounds a week went for my keep and another three pounds went towards repaying Paul, the £150 he had lent me to buy my first car. The money saved from my paper round had turned out to be just enough to pay for my driving lessons, which I received from Mum's brother, my Uncle Joe.

Rease Heath Agricultural College in Nantwich was where David wanted to go when he left school, but Dad wouldn't let him. Instead, he worked at Bonells for a couple of years and then, even though he didn't have to, joined the RAF, to get away, as he saw it.

Paul was also accepted for Rease Heath. He had always reared poultry in the back garden at Newholme and seemed to spend more time at the farm next door than he did at home, but he came up against the same strong opposition. Instead, he went to work in the village Co-op, where he subsequently became manager.

At least, when I left college, I managed to get a job in my dream career - or so I thought at the time.

8

So, standing next to a hearse outside a church, collecting the names of mourners and the list of people they were representing, became part of my reporting duties. "Names sell papers." Then, there were the parish councils, village fetes, unusually shaped vegetables and talented pets! This was journalism at the sharp end.

In those early days I foolishly told my colleagues when my Dad dreamt the winner of the Grand National. Not only that, but he had done the same, years before, when he predicted Battleship would win, which it duly did. Sounds like a story, someone said.

'Oh no, not my Dad. You don't know him,' I muttered. 'If his prediction comes off maybe, but, otherwise, no.' You can see how much I knew about newspapers.

Word went around and a reporter from the Daily Express heard about it. He came and chatted, having hardly spoken to me before.

When I got home that night, the said reporter had been around to visit my parents, telling them how well I was doing on the newspaper - and then asking about the Grand National.

I can't even remember the name of the horse that my Dad dreamt had won, only that it didn't! He also dreamt that the favourite, Two Springs (I can still remember that name) had fallen three fences from home. That didn't happen either.

There was a front-page story in the Daily Express on the morning of the race about Dad, saying how the whole of the village was excited because they thought he had dreamt the winner of the National again. Actually, up until that point, I don't think anyone knew anything about his dream, apart from the Daily Express readers.

A colleague who had been visiting friends, saw the London edition of the Express that morning. The story had been promoted to headline news there. "Dreamer Fred," it proclaimed. Mercifully, Dreamer Fred never saw that edition.

He didn't complain about the story he did see, though. Nor did he seem to mind the prediction hadn't come true. He didn't even back the horse he had dreamt about!

For once, I suspect Dad was proud that I'd got that job as a reporter, after all. Not that he would ever have said so.

9

So, she is just about to start baking when there's a knock at the back door. Wiping her hands on her pinny, she pats her hair and goes to answer it, squeezing past the table which, with blanket folded over one end, doubles as her ironing board. She is careful of the upturned iron which is still hot from when she used it earlier.

Adjusting her glasses, she catches sight of her reflection in the mirror over the kitchen range, seeing the flour highlights she has added to either side of her ginger hair. She sends flour billowing in the air around her as she pats frantically at it, then takes a breath before she undoes the Yale lock on the door.

'Elsie?' she says.

Elsie stands there. She is younger than Joyce and has a glow to her cheeks. Joyce just has some redness from the heat of the iron on hers.

'Joyce. Fred in?'

My mother shakes her head and smiles. 'How are you?'

Elsie laughs. 'How do you think?'

My mother blushes at the sharpness of the reply. There is hardly a trace of recognition in Elsie's face, as if they were suddenly strangers, those conversations and countless cups of tea never having been shared.

Elsie stands a good yard or so from the door, avoiding my mother's eyes. 'Perhaps you could give him a message then. Tell him, I've not had my money.' she says patting her swollen stomach. 'Soon be more, of course.'

My mother nods and turns away.

'Tell him, I don't want to have to come around again. Don't forget.'

As if she could, no matter how much she wanted to. She grips her hands together and conjures up a faint smile. 'I'll tell him.'

Not that she did. Any mention of the visit would have only led to a fresh argument, and she could do without any more of them.

She knows what's been going on, of course, even if it is never spoken about; knows about the biscuit tin under the bath, the one only her husband is allowed to open. In view of his intense dislike of banks and how he always said he wouldn't trust them with his money, she had an idea what might be inside.

Then one day, when he didn't know she was standing behind him, she had seen exactly what was in there. A hand went to her lips to suppress a gasp.

10

So, the noises in the washhouse have been going on for some days now, hammering and sawing. The door is firmly shut and the quivering cobwebs on the inside of the small window make it difficult to see inside.

He can make out the outline of his father, standing with his back to him. There's a hammer in his hand and he is working on something in front of him. In the far corner, the copper-bottomed bowl set into the top of the brick chimney boiler is covered in tools.

His father turns, as if sensing someone is watching. Next, the door bursts open and he stands there, sweating, hammer still in hand. 'You keep away from here, until I tell you different,' he says.

'When will that be?' David asks.

'When I tell you different.'

The noises continue in the washhouse for some days afterwards, until there is a sudden cold spell. Then, they move inside the house, to the downstairs bathroom.

'Am I banned from there now?' David asks.

All is revealed when Christmas morning arrives. He wakes early and scratches at the ice on the inside of his bedroom window. There has been a hard frost overnight, but no snow. The surrounding fields are sprinkled seasonally white as is the roof of the outbuildings below.

He waits impatiently until he hears a noise from his parent's bedroom and then calls out, 'Can I get up yet?'

'Stay where you are until I tell you different,' his father calls back.

After a few minutes he hears footsteps going downstairs and scratches more ice from the windowpane. There are footprints in the frost on the back yard now and the door to *the washhouse is open. A moment later his father emerges and waves for him to come down.*

David hurtles downstairs and runs outside where his father stands before the open door. His eyes widen when he sees what his father has made for him inside. Just what he wanted. A model railway. As well as the train set, there is a station with waiting rooms and two platforms, each lined on one side by a picket fence, made from what looked like, shaped lollipop sticks.

He smiles almost as much as his father does. His mother is standing at the back door smiling too. 'Merry Christmas,' *she says. That year it was.*

My Dad made something for me once. Just like with David's station, it was completely unexpected.

In my early teens, various hobbies had been dabbled at, with a view to making me rich and famous or, at least, guaranteeing my place on Opportunity Knocks.

First, there had been magic. The mystical ghost tubes made from cornflake packets, the black bag with hidden compartment that made an imitation egg appear and disappear, (not confident enough to use a real one!) and the grubby pack of playing cards. How many times had my mother been bombarded with requests to, "Pick a card"?

A brief dalliance with ventriloquism followed, but that had been given short shift. An inherent difficulty in keeping my mouth shut! Then, it was puppets.

My troupe of Pelham Puppets was built up from Christmas and birthday presents from my parents and brother Paul. With these trusty marionettes, complete with their coloured strings (so you knew what you were pulling!), I performed at a few children's parties.

"The Petite Puppet Company", I wrote on the hardboard frontage of my make-shift stage. During the performances, the kids used to creep closer and closer, until they could look up under the façade and see me pulling the strings. I made faces at them to go away which they seemed to enjoy more than the puppet show they were supposed to be watching.

That piece of wood was later used by my Dad to help make a false ceiling to insulate the freezing outside toilet. "The Petite Puppet Company" staring down at you as you sat there, contemplating life.

One of the puppets was a rather grand-looking wolf. He walked on two legs, not four, wore check trousers, a black cape lined in red and had over-large heavy white hands and no elbows. A natural pianist, I decided, if only there was a piano for him to play. My Dad must have been listening.

A few weeks later he presented me with a baby grand-style piano. It had an opening top, was painted black and sat rather awkwardly on three short barley twist legs, salvaged from the discarded back of the sideboard. Thoughtfully, foam rubber had been put on the keyboard to soak up the noise when the wolf heavy handedly set about playing. It was great. And was, also, the only thing Dad ever made for me. Should have taken better care of it.

Like David's present, it was a complete surprise. He remembers the year of his train set as being his best Christmas ever. Mum even had a sip of sherry and a fit of the giggles that year.

David had seen one of the picket fencing sticks from the station lying on the bathroom floor, in the days leading up to Christmas, and wondered what it was.

The bathroom had always been a place of interest to David, if not the bath itself. He liked to crawl under the claw feet of the bath and hide, tormenting any spiders which tried to run away when he disturbed their cobwebs. It was there he found a battered biscuit tin, pushed right up against the outside wall.

Pulling it out from under the bath, he was surprised there wasn't any dust on it. When he carefully prised open the lid, his eyes fell open in amazement.

The tin was full, crammed right to the top, with white five-pound notes.

11

So, he hears his mother's sobs from outside and gingerly peers in through the kitchen window. The air inside is steamy with a kettle boiling away, seemingly unattended.

He tries to be quiet, but a stone or something is stuck under the bottom of the door, causing it to scrape across the tiled floor as it opens.

His mother turns, wiping away a tear with the corner of her pinny. 'It's nothing,' she says.

What looks like blood is on the floor, a red smear with a partial shoeprint in it. There's a bowl in front of her on the table with something inside.

'It wasn't meant to be,' she says. 'Go along outside and play.'

She drapes a tea towel over the bowl and takes it to the bathroom, trying to shield what is inside as she goes. But, as she turns in the doorway, he catches a glimpse.

David is only seven and, at first, is not sure what he is looking at. It looks like a perfect little baby, but only two or three inches long.

He has a tear in his eye as he remembers it now. 'It looked perfect and had little arms and legs, everything. I don't know what happened to it, but I can't forget the image of that perfectly formed little baby.'

12

So, my father calls me outside. 'Hurry up or you'll miss it,' he says, leading me by the hand to the front corner of the garden.

A giant Heinkel plane is flying really low over the ground, so low it has to speed up and increase height just to clear the line of poplar trees at the side of the road outside our house. I duck down as it feels, surely, that the plane will brush the top of my head. The noise is overwhelming now.

We watch as the plane chugs away, a trail of bullets from the pursuing RAF Spitfires snaking across the night sky behind it, this time high and wide of the target.

We often watch these scrimmages in the air, my father and me. This time the enemy escapes, but one night a German plane is shot down. There's an explosion. Then, away in the distance, the sky lights up. A few seconds later, two parachutes open, floating down beneath the wreckage, illuminated by the flames.

The next day my father takes me to see the giant crater left in the ground. We're not the only would-be sightseers, but the Ministry of Defence has already been and cleared the wreckage away by the time we arrive. Well, not quite all of it, for amongst the grass, I spot a fragment of green aluminium at my feet.

'David,' my father calls me over to him.

My find goes furtively into my pocket before anyone sees. It was just a scrap of metal, but I kept it for years.

Later I learnt that the pilots made it safely to the ground, but their freedom had been short-lived. A couple of days later the Home Guard had captured them in nearby Hankelow.

Dad had been too old to fight in the war himself. Instead, he served in the auxiliary fire service. I didn't get to see his service badge and medal as David had given them away to a boyhood friend who was also a fireman. 'I thought he might like them,' David told me when I asked him why.

The Germans used to regularly drop incendiary bombs and mines on barns in the area and Dad and his colleagues in the Auxiliary Fire Service, nicknamed them, Firelighters.

David remembers his father telling him how, once, when they had been dealing with a burning barn, he had suddenly been "taken short", as he called it, and went behind the hedge to relieve himself.

When he got up, trousers still around his ankles, he looked down and saw one of the explosive devices which he had almost sat, not to mention shat, on.

'He said he had never run so fast. He could hear it ticking.'

13

So, throughout the war a stream of evacuees came to stay at Newholme. Groups of them would arrive in the village hall, waiting to be divided up amongst local families, looking lost with their names written on tags tied to the buttonholes of their coats, clutching their little suitcases or bags.

Most memorable for David were the twins evacuated from Guernsey when the Germans invaded the island. 'I can still remember their names. Ernest and Edwin Ingreville. They stayed quite a long time. They were good, they were.'

After the war, David, and all the children from the village whose parents had taken in evacuees were invited over for a two-week holiday in Guernsey, all expenses paid. 'We went swimming, and to the pictures and funfair. We had a great time.'

Before the twins, there had been three youngsters evacuated from a bomb-ravaged part of Merseyside. There were two brothers and a sister. They shared the cylinder cupboard bedroom at Newholme whilst David was relegated to the smaller box room. He was about 9 or 10 at the time and remembers waking one morning to find the young girl, who was the same age, trying to get into bed with him.

Mother had a fit. She had already noticed things going missing around the house and seen the boys burying a tin in the garden. At first, she had feared it might be the tin from under the bath, but it wasn't. There was money in it though. They didn't stay long.

She had tried her best. At Christmas time, they told her they didn't believe in Santa Claus because they had never had any presents. Well, he came visiting them that year!

On Christmas morning, they couldn't believe their eyes when they saw their stockings hanging from the ends of the mantlepiece.

'She gave them lots of things,' remembers David. 'They gave me impetigo.'

14

So, the back door opens. A glance up at the clock, as she's been worried where he was. He didn't usually stay out late. Putting down her knitting, she gets up from the settee and goes into the kitchen.

'Whatever are you doing standing there in the dark?' she asks, switching on the light.

Fred is in the doorway, leaning heavily against it for support, his eyes red and puffy. He sniffs to stop a tear falling down his cheek.

'Whatever's the matter?' she says, leading him through to the front room.

He stops and looks at his wife for a moment. 'She's finished with me,' he says.

Letting go of his arm, my mother steadies herself. Words won't come and, instead, she stares at her clenched fingers, makes them straighten the antimacassar on the back of the settee. It takes both her hands.

'He's back from the war and she said it couldn't go on any longer.' He's sobbing now. 'I didn't know what to do. I found myself down by the canal, walking up and down the towpath for what seemed like hours, peering into the water. I didn't know if it was worth carrying on.'

My mother stifles a sob. She'd never seen him like this before, never seen him display such emotion. What exactly is she supposed to say? How does he think she feels? She looks anywhere except at her husband.

'At one point I nearly jumped in,' he says, slumping against her.

His arms go around her, for the first time in a long time, and she freezes for a moment. Then, she puts her arms around him, loosely at first, and then her grip grows tighter.

They stay like that for a long time, locked in each other's arms. Neither says any more.

15

So, there is the sound of a baby crying. Paul has just been born in the bedroom above and one of my mother's sisters is with her to help.

In the front room below, sitting on the old saggy settee with the coming-together of cushions in the middle, sits my father alongside a neighbour, a little too closely alongside for my Auntie Muriel's liking.

She lets out a heavy sigh as she passes through the front room and struggles to open the door to the stairs with her arms already full. No-one makes any effort to get up and help her.

David remembers the time he'd seen his father in the front bar of the Lord Combermere pub in the village, sitting alongside the said neighbour, laughing and joking. Seeing them sit there now, with a smirk on their faces, makes him look away and go outside.

This might have been one of the contributing factors for what happened when I was born three years later.

My mother is pacing the floor. It's nearly time but, still no-one has arrived. They might still come, she supposed, even though it was unlikely. It looked like there was to be a family boycott of the christening which was due to take place in the Methodist chapel at Chapel End in just over an hour's time.

'There's got to be god parents,' my mother says between tears. 'Someone has got to be there.'

Fred disappears and comes back ten minutes later. 'Down the road say they'll do it.'

My mother is momentarily reassured and then realises.
'But.... you can't ask them!'
'No one else. You want Godparents or not?'

So, there were Godparents in the end, but it always rankled my mother who she had to rely on.

Looking back, you wonder why my parents stayed together in view of all the things that happened, but couples did in those days, didn't they?

David remembers arguments between them, though not what they were about. There would be raised voices. 'He would swear at her sometimes, even called her a bitch on one occasion, but he never hit her.'

There were no real quarrels when I was growing up. There was a distance between them I felt, and not just because Dad always sat in "his" chair and Mum always on the settee when they were watching television. My place would be on the settee between them. They didn't seem to talk to each other much, certainly not when the television was on, anyway.

Years earlier, there was one time when Mum decided to leave. She packed a case and took David with her, but returned home a couple of hours later, having only got as far as a neighbour's house down the road. Whether Dad even realised she had gone or not is unclear.

Ironic, that the only place she could think to go when she left, was the same neighbour who David had seen cuddling with his father in the pub in the village; the one whose son later became my godfather.

16

So, we're looking through some old pictures, my mother and me, when we come across an old photograph with curled up edges. A darkly dressed figure is standing in a poorly lit room, seemingly standing guard over a pot plant with spiky leaves. It looks very funereal, like one of those old grainy pictures you see taken at a séance.

'That's Gran Savill,' says Mum. 'Alice.' She looks closely at the picture for a moment and then adds, 'She tried to push me down the stairs once.'

I look at her, but she doesn't elaborate and puts the photographs away, back into the sideboard drawer, pushing it firmly shut.

'Leave the door...'

It was too late. Alice closed the bedroom door behind her, even though she'd seen Joyce standing by the airing cupboard with an armful of clothes.

Joyce took a breath and exchanged the clothes for towels to take down to the bathroom. 'Could you open the door please?' she called out.

There was no response, so she fumbled with the door handle and stepped out onto the narrow landing where Alice was standing looking out of the window, across the fields to the farm opposite.

'If you could just let me pass,' Joyce said, but Alice made no attempt to move.

As she squeezed around her, Joyce's foot slipped on the stair on the turn at the top of the staircase and fell over sidewards onto Alice. Alice reacted instinctively and pushed her away, sending Joyce tottering forward towards the steep flight of stairs.

Feeling herself falling, she let out a scream, dropped the towels and grabbed desperately at the landing curtains to hang onto. There was a ripping sound as several curtain hooks gave way.

'You, you pushed me,' she said incredulously.

Alice shook her head. 'It was you who pushed me.' And with that, set off down the stairs, walking over the newly aired towels now draped in her path.

Neither of my parents spoke much about the London side of the family, as my mother called it. After Dad's father was run over and killed in the capital by a double decker bus or tram (depending on which relative you choose to believe), Alice had upped and gone to Canada when Dad was a boy. She had left him and his sister, Dorothy, to be brought up by an aunt. What happened in Canada was never spoken about.

'We called her Mrs Pritchard,' my Auntie Mary once said to me rather puzzlingly, when referring to the Gran-I-never-knew.

Only very recently did I see another picture of Alice. It was a group photograph taken at my parent's wedding. I had previously only seen the bride and groom picture, the one hanging on the kitchen wall at Newholme.

In the group shot, Gran Savill is pictured to the right of the groom, sitting on a chair holding an impressive spray of flowers. She has her hair pinned back in the fashion of the day and looks a bit like Queen Mary. No hint of a smile.

After Fred and Joyce were married, Alice sold the shop in Audlem and moved back to London. When she returned after the war, minus any money, she moved in with my parents.

She arrived at Newholme when David was about thirteen. She looked like an old lady to him, very tall and very thin, wizen even, and given to wearing a lot of black.

She took up residence in the cylinder cupboard back bedroom, relegating David to the boxroom again. She didn't bring many possessions with her, but there was an engraved box with a maple leaf on the lid.

He and his Gran would play cards for hours and during their conversations it soon became apparent to him that she didn't like his mother. 'She thought mother wasn't good enough for her Fred, even though she was a farmer's daughter herself.'

Alice encouraged Fred to go out for a drink in the evening, leaving her and Joyce at home together in those pre-television days, presumably to scowl at each other over their knitting.

When her health failed, Alice was admitted to the Barony Cottage hospital in Nantwich. Dad used to visit regularly, occasionally taking David with him. My mother never went once.

Dad had bought a triple plot in the village cemetery, for him, Joyce, and his mother. A proper plot away from the parish graves near the hedge, with proper views across to Moss Hall. They lay there now, the three of them, one atop the other.

'And to think, one day I will have to lie on top of her in my grave,' my mother once said to me tearfully.

Alice's presence in the plot is unmarked. One thing my mother did achieve – a wish not to have Alice mentioned on the gravestone. Or maybe it was just because they never had the money for a headstone at the time?

When my Dad died in 1977, he was next into the plot, meaning that when my mother died thirteen years later, she did not have to lie directly on top of Alice. She would have been glad about that. Dad keeping them apart again, once and for all.

17

So, at the bottom of the Big Bank, down an even narrower roadway, lived my grandparents.

Rose Cottage was semi-detached with a long back garden and flowers matching its name growing around the front door. When my Grandad retired, they moved there from Bridge House. From the front garden of Rose Cottage, you could see Bridge House up on the hill, away to the left.

In the back garden of the cottage was an earth lavatory. I don't remember ever using it. You didn't, unless you were desperate.

It was bad enough having to go at home, where we had a similar arrangement. The thought of that Izal toilet paper still makes me cringe, but that was better, just about, than newspaper. Oh, the embarrassment if the school bus came back in the afternoon when the shit-wagon (so called by all the kids on the bus) was still doing collections outside your house. Mainstream drainage did not arrive in these parts until well into the 1960's.

Bridge House, on the other hand, had its own septic tank. Very posh. David remembers it was emptied by local celebrity Blaster Bates, better known latterly for his demolition work and raconteurial skills. There is a family story of him reciting a risqué ditty during one emptying, much to the embarrassment of all who heard it.

Strangely, the outside privy at Rose Cottage, started to feature in my childhood dreams. It became my safe place, my Tardis to rescue me. In times of trouble, it would miraculously appear, like the aforementioned time machine, where-ever I was in my dreams, in this world or the next. All I had to do to escape whatever was chasing me, was lift the metal catch, push open the wooden planked door and open my eyes.

Once, whatever was chasing me grabbed my ankle just as I reached the door, pulled me back, stopped me from getting inside and opening my eyes, stopped me escaping. No more sleep for me that night!

In the summer, the back garden of Rose Cottage would be full of vegetables, uniform rows of wigwam-like canes supporting peas and broad beans, cabbages spilling out onto the path, stretching all the way down to the railway line. Steam trains used to run to Market Drayton in those days, before Beeching had his way.

A simple wooden platform served as the Cox Bank halt. Mum used to get very nervous that the train wouldn't stop for her and would wave frantically at the approaching engine. Then, coming back home, she would worry that she wasn't in the right compartment to get off. The platform was only one carriage long.

The train was a rare luxury. I can picture one journey, sitting on a moquette covered seat in our own compartment, steam billowing past, mother telling me to get my head back inside and close the window.

Usually if we went to Drayton, it would be on the twice daily market day bus that ran on a Wednesday and which we could catch outside our house.

Mum always used to worry about journeys on public transport. Visiting David and Joy in Crewe was a fraught experience. It involved a change of bus and, consequently, speculation that the connection could be missed. Then, connection made, Mum would always stand up two stops early and get off at the stop before the one she wanted, in case she missed the one she did!

Every week my mother used to walk the mile or so down to Rose Cottage to see her parents and help with the housework. Every week, that is, unless one of her three sisters were visiting. 'Not next week, Joyce. Gladys is coming,' Gran would say.

In Gran's Sunday best front room, there was an organ with giant pedals covered in bits of carpet, that you pressed down, almost like you were driving it. Mum would play when we visited, usually something religious-sounding, whatever music was at hand. She couldn't play without music. Sometimes I'd go in and listen, as that was the only way I would be allowed in there. It was dark and smelt of polish.

There were a pair of rearing spelter horses at either end of the organ and, on a low table on a lacey mat, a big well-worn leather-bound family bible with metal fastening which I wasn't allowed to touch. The future ownership of the horses and bible were the source of much discussion when my grandparents moved into a council bungalow in the village.

My sister-in-law remembers a rug being pulled from under her as an undisclosed voice proclaimed, "I was promised that." Mum didn't receive anything, as far as I'm aware. She still went to help when her parents moved to the council bungalow in Audlem - unless one of her sisters was expected, of course.

On a Saturday morning, I would go down to Gran's who would send me to the betting office with her shilling each-way bets. As a reward I was treated to a sixpence each-way bet on a horse of my choosing. I was well under-age, but never had any trouble placing the bets. In the afternoon we would sit and watch the races on television.

My Gran loved horses with Red in their name. Red Alligator being a particular favourite. Pity she died before Red Rum came along.

18

So, thinking back, there was one occasion when Mum and Dad went out together, as a couple as it were.

A local farmer's wife had arranged a bus trip to the cinema in nearby Hanley to see The Sound of Music. Mum bought tickets and, a little reluctantly, Dad went along.

They loved it and both talked enthusiastically about it for days afterwards. Dad trying to remember the songs. 'That Julie Andrews, she's a good singer. Don't let anyone tell you different'. Mum buying the sheet music to play for herself.

We never went on holiday. Well, there was one time: a week in Abergele. Mum, Paul, me and Joy with her young daughter, Lynn. David was working. Dad didn't come.

Our caravan site wasn't that far from the sea. You couldn't see it, or hear it, but you could smell it. You had to climb a bridge over the main railway line to get to the stony beach and, if a train was coming, you had to hurry before you were covered in fumes.

Money ran out and we only had enough to buy two packets of crisps to share at the station on the way home. One of them was the newly introduced cheese and onion flavour which, up to that point, I hadn't liked. It started to grow on me.

We did go out as a family together once, with both my Mum and Dad. Dad even organised it!

We didn't have a car, so he got one of his friends to drive us up to Blackpool. There was me, Paul, Mum, and Dad. It was a school day which Mum wasn't too pleased about, but it was either then or else not at all. On the way there we stopped for petrol and Dad bought me a bar of chocolate.

Mum and Dad didn't go on any of the rides, but me and Paul did. We played the slot machines, rolled pennies down chutes to try and dislodge mountains of overhanging coins and fired pistols with suction-cap bullets at targets.

At the end of the day, we ate chips out of newspaper and then joined in the long queue to drive back down the front to see the illuminations. It was late when we got back.

The trip to Blackpool came after Dad won £50 on the horses, quite a sum in those days. He didn't gamble a lot, just on a Saturday. He'd stake his modest "investment", as he called it, in the tiny wooden shed which served as the village's betting shop. Sometimes, I'd see him, walking across from the Lord Combermere pub, when I went to put on Gran's bets.

He only went for a drink Saturday and Sunday lunchtimes and never came home drunk. But, on a Sunday, he always arrived back after the rest of us had finished our Sunday dinner. He had his reheated on a tray in front of the television.

19

'So, drain as much tea as you can from the cup, then turn it around three times. No, that way. To the left. Now, quickly turn it over onto the saucer.'

The wide-eyed child opposite does as he's told. I stand at his side and nod approval.

Word that my mother read tea leaves had spread around and one of my friends wanted to have his fortune told. As did I, of course.

Expectations always far exceeded what the tea leaves delivered, courtesy of my Mum. It didn't stop us persisting in the hope of being informed of good luck or untold wealth coming our way. Sometimes, I'd ask for a second reading if nothing good came up first time around.

Once, she saw a shape in the leaves, an eagle if memory serves, and warned me to be careful. I didn't pay much attention. It was just the good bits I wanted to hear.

Anyway, on the day of the eagle warning, I promptly went up the road and fell into the cattle grid leading to one of the farms. Stuck by the kneecaps, the farmer had to come and prise the metal bars apart with a wooden pole to get me out, a little sore, but otherwise unhurt. Tea leaf warnings were always heeded after that.

We weren't allowed to talk whilst Mum peered inside the china cup. (It had to be china!) There was certainly a sense of ceremony to the reading which added to the whole thing. She might even have drawn the curtains. When it was quiet, she would turn the cup, this way and that, until something materialised in the soggy mass of tea leaves smeared up the sides of the cup.

The readings always took place when my Dad wasn't at home and were conducted solemnly around the kitchen table. We didn't go into the front room until the evening.

There were only two downstairs rooms at Newholme. The kitchen and the front room. A door led off the front room to the box-sized hallway with the never-opened front door, shrouded in a heavy curtain. Opposite, the staircase led steeply upwards.

In pride of place in the front room, as well as the piano (of which more later), was the television set. The whole family gathered in the front room the evening the man from Breeden and Middleton came to "install" the rented set. I was seven and he gave me a metal bolt from the packing case as a keepsake.

Breeden and Middleton's! That was where our very 1950's looking three-piece suite, on spindly wooden legs with metal castors, came from. My father nearly had a cardiac when it was delivered. He never stopped complaining about it, saying it wouldn't last five minutes. He was quite content to keep the baggy old settee with the coming-together of cushions in the middle and springs sagging down to the ground.

My mother bought the red and white vision in vinyl on the never-never. Dad didn't approve. Up until then we hadn't had anything unless we could afford to pay for it.

We went into Breeden and Middleton's not long afterwards and, to my mother's horror, there was a shiny-topped dining room table and chairs with a ticket attached declaring, "Sold, Savill" on it. There might even have been a matching sideboard, complete with inset clock on the back, to go with it.

An asthma attack threatened. 'I never. I didn't,' my mother wheezed.

My sister-in-law calmed her down and cancelled whatever it was Mum had unwittingly agreed to. My father never knew about that. We didn't go to Breeden and Middleton's again. Nor did we have anything else "on tick," which meant we went without.

My Mum did buy a brand-new twin tub washing machine, though, when an insurance policy matured. £30, it cost. A Rolls twin tub. She was so chuffed.

'It's a Rolls,' she would say, like it was the equivalent in the washing machine world to a Rolls in the automotive one. The firm went bust shortly after she bought it.

She would stand and watch in fascination at it juddering up and down as it did the weekly wash. You had to manually transfer the soaking wet washing from the washing tub into the drying tub with a pair of great big wooden tongs. A bucket at the side of the machine caught any water that came out on the spin cycle. There always seemed to be residue water left in the bucket. My pet hamster fell in it once when it escaped from its cage. Luckily it could swim.

Mum was so proud of that machine. She used to put a cloth over the Formica top to protect it from the sun.

20

So, my mother's only escape from domestic drudgery was her piano. Her pride and joy, which was polished religiously every week. A gleaming dark mahogany veneered upright which stood in the front room, out of direct sunlight. It had been a present from my father in the early years of their marriage, in the days of the white five-pound notes, no doubt.

Mum was an accomplished player and gave piano lessons. The clicking of the metronome, standing in its wooden case on an embroidered dioly on top of the piano, was a regular sound, whilst the knitting needle resting at the back of the keys was a familiar sight. The needle was used rather like a conductor's baton, waved up and down to point at the music, rather than to tap hesitant fingers.

A constant stream of children used to arrive after school for their lessons. Mum used to charge two and sixpence an hour (pre decimal), latterly rising to 50p and, then, a whole pound! There would be an extra charge of 5p in the winter to help pay for the coal for the fire.

In the early days, our pet spaniel, Tina, threatened to dent the takings by chewing her way through two pairs of Wellingtons, left inside the back door by pupils having their lessons.

My Dad arrived home about half past five, sometimes whilst the lessons were still going on. The first thing he did was switch on the television, leaning forward, turning the volume down low, as the music lesson progressed a few feet away. Sometimes, if the television was too loud, it would warrant a stern, "Fred!" from my mother.

She continued giving music lessons right up until the time she died at the age of 81. There was, latterly, a framed photograph of Mum sitting at a piano, surrounded by her pupils, when they gave a concert in Audlem Public Hall. It stood in pride of place on top of her piano.

When she died, she left her treasured instrument to one of her pupils as neither my brothers nor I had shown any interest in it.

My piano certificates are probably still around somewhere, but now I can't play a note. Burnt out by eleven. Mind you, I did buy a guitar in my late teens, taught myself three chords, wrote a few songs with lines that didn't rhyme and managed to achieve that long-held ambition of getting an audition for Opportunity Knocks.

It was at some big hotel in Blackpool. A friend's mother went with me. 'Well, it was better than I thought it was going to be,' she said afterwards.

I sang a self-penned song called, Who's the Winner Now? Still waiting to hear back from them.

21

So, if it was Saturday, it must have been the butcher I'm thinking about. If not a Saturday, then it could have been any of the numerous other grocery delivery men who came to our back door. All the village shops used to have delivery vans in those days.

Monday was Mr Averill's night. He usually came in the evening around six o'clock. Mum had to close the door between the kitchen and front room because Dad would be watching the news and you weren't allowed to talk when the news was on.

Something was always purchased from Mr Averill, whether Mum needed it or not. She didn't want to disappoint him. I liked to go out and peer into the back of his van, an Alladin's cave, lined with shelves packed high with packets, tins and boxes of brightly coloured sweets.

Tuesday was Mr Allen's day. His van was bigger and full of freshly baked bread. Sometimes, Mum used to buy me a small-coiled loaf - can't remember what they were called, a Nimble loaf maybe? I'd eat it whilst it was still warm. Better than sweets. A treat though, so not to be repeated too often.

The Co-op had the biggest van of all, but that was the only one that didn't call, that is, until my brother, Paul, went to work there. The van started calling after that.

The milkman, of course, did his doorstop deliveries of the silver topped bottles six days a week. At the weekend, we had one gold top bottle as well, which you had to shake first, so you didn't get all the cream. It would really upset Mum if you didn't. Automatically shaking milk bottles is still a habit of mine to this day, long after the demise of the silver and gold tops.

Sometimes, in the winter, the bottles would be covered in snow on the doorstep, the silver and gold tops pushed up into the air above the frozen liquid inside, like miniature ice lollies.

Saturday was the butcher's day to call. He brought the weekly joint of beef, lamb, or pork, for our Sunday roast dinner, as well as sausages and bacon for our Sunday morning breakfast.

On the day I'm thinking of, I was descending the stairs when the sound of a little squeal, a sort of giggle came from our kitchen. It wasn't the usual sort of noise to be coming from there, so I went to investigate.

My mother was manoeuvring herself around the kitchen table pursued by the delivery man who was smiling and laughing. He said her name, Joyce, with what sounded like a question mark after it.

Mum did her usual straightening-of-the-hair thing and said 'thank you' very primly and the delivery man smiled back and let himself out of the back door. 'See you next week.'

It was all probably entirely innocent, but Mum coloured up good and proper.

You know, thinking back, didn't we have extra sausages that week?

22

So, there it was on the front page of the local evening newspaper, the Shropshire Star. The 28th ^{of} March 1985. 'Double death at Farmhouse,' read the front-page headline. Bridge House and the Edwards's were in the news.

The report was the first time I discovered that there had originally been three sisters living at Bridge House. One had died a couple of years before the tragedy.

According to the newspaper report, police had been called to the property by a concerned coalman who suspected something was wrong.

Younger sister, Amy (77) was found lying on the kitchen floor and George (85) and his elder sister, Jessie (91) were found slumped in chairs in the living room semi-conscious.

Amy was confirmed dead on arrival at hospital and George died later the same day. Postmortems revealed Amy died of heart failure and George of hypothermia. Jessie received treatment for hypothermia but recovered.

News went around the village like wildfire. There were rumours of antique pots found, stuffed with money, at the isolated farmhouse. Not that any money was subsequently found after a burglary cleared out most of the valuables.

Jessie moved into a nursing home in the village, the former grammar school which was latterly the secondary modern school I attended for a year, before it closed, and the pupils transferred to Shavington.

My brother, Paul, visited Jessie regularly. I was working in London at the time but did visit once.

She had her own downstairs room, part of the one where, in my schooldays, Domestic Science had been taught. She was curled up in an armchair where she apparently preferred to sleep, rather than in her bed. Paul introduced me, but she didn't say anything, and we left after a few minutes.

When she died, Jessie left my brother and mother something in her will.

'Nothing for me then,' I had joked.

Paul managed one of his what I now call "half-brother story" looks. 'Said you'd never done a day's hard work in your life.'

23

So, it's the early hours of the morning and Paul is woken by the sound of his Dad calling. 'Paul. Quick! It's your mother.'

Paul had often been sent for the doctor in the middle of the night when Mum had a bad asthma attack. He would cycle down to the doctor's house and throw pebbles at the window if knocking at the door failed to rouse anyone.

'She's not breathing,' Dad says, gently shaking her arm and, when there's no response, shakes a little harder. Not sure what to do, he puts his ear to her mouth.

He's seen it done enough times on television, in Your Life in Their Hands and Emergency Ward 10, so, in desperation, he breathes into her mouth, softly at first and then more urgently.

He looks at her face in-between his breaths into her lungs. 'Come on Joyce. Come on.'

For a moment he's distracted. A thought runs through his mind. How long is it since he kissed her? How long since she kissed him?

He shakes the thoughts away and starts again. There's a murmur as Joyce stirs. Paul comes back saying someone is on their way.

'She's breathing now.' Dad lets out a deep breath. 'I gave her the kiss of life,' he says. 'I think I did it right.'

Dad had always seemed so healthy. As Mum's health grew worse, he looked after her without complaint. Paying back for his earlier transgressions? Who knows? But he was there at her bedside when needed.

Then, quite unexpectedly, he was diagnosed with lung cancer. He was a heavy smoker in his younger days, but I don't remember him smoking that much, at least, not in the house. One cherished photograph is of him in the back yard, leaning against the fence, in his shirt and braces, with a cigarette in his hand.

We didn't dare tell him it was the "big C," as they used to call it in those days. He wasn't the sort to fight it. Or so we decided for him.

He didn't go into hospital and now it was Mum's turn to do the caring. Joy came and stayed over to help look after him in his final days. There was a nurse who visited as well after Dad developed a bedsore. David remembers his father crying out in pain when she tried to turn him over.

Mum and Dad had moved in with Paul when he bought a bungalow in the village. They hadn't been in their new home many months before Dad died. 'We moved in on the Good Friday and he died in the October,' Paul remembers.

One of the last things Dad did was ask David to give him a shave, a good old fashioned wet shave. 'He'd never asked me to do that before. I gave him a good shave.'

There were tears and grief, of course, but in the years that followed Dad's death, Mum entered a new phase of her life. She went to stay with her sisters and had trips out with them.

She kept me well chronicled of her goings-on in the weekly letters she sent to me when I moved to a job in London. My move in 1980 coincided with a series of bombings by the IRA in the capital which I was reporting on. But she was just as concerned about me getting my pocket picked, or the trains being delayed when I came back home to visit.

Made me smile, reading a bundle of her letters from that time, funny, heart-warming and often quite random.

"...you don't go out to the pubs on your own, do you? Things seem to happen to people down there..."

"...thanks for the snaps. It would have been a very good one of you if the light hadn't got in..."

"...I now have eleven pupils ... I love having them, something to look forward to and a change of conversation..."

"...you should ask the name of the pilot when you go to Germany. It would be lovely to find out it was your cousin..."

"...do look after yourself. I am always thinking of you..."

24

So, I moved back to Audlem to live in the house where David had been born – Ingleside. Strange how that happened.

Whilst showing my partner, Michael, around Audlem, we drove past Ingleside. It was a two bedroomed semi-detached cottage, directly on the side of the road. Ingleside was written on a plaster plaque in the brickwork on the front.

Further along, on the other side of the lane was another pair of cottages, Sunnyside. As there was a For Sale sign outside Ingleside, we stopped. The front door was wide open, so we stepped inside.

Our inspection was cut short when a man appeared at the doorway demanding to know how we had got inside. The door had been firmly locked, he maintained. Michael and I looked at each other. Must have been meant, as they say.

Having sold my flat in Hampton Wick, I had moved in with Michael and so, perhaps in a rash moment, decided to buy Ingleside. Compared to London prices it was dead cheap. Originally, it was going to be a country retreat and then, later, after getting a job in Stafford, I moved up permanently. Michael took early retirement and came up a year or so later.

I gave up my job and together, we set up an antique shop in Nantwich. Not exactly antique, it was art deco, a passion for which we had developed together. It was the early 1980's and, at a time when blue and white china and oak furniture was the norm, art deco was a new concept to some in those parts of the world. One of the first people inside the shop in Welsh Row wanted to buy a paintbrush.

Mum loved to visit the shop and, was among the first of many to say, "Oh, we used to have one of those."

Mum and Paul would come around to visit, Mum enjoying seeing Ingleside again after all those years, pointing out the spot where David had been born in the front bedroom.

Occasionally, they would stay for a meal. 'It's very nice, but the vegetables could have done with a bit more salt,' she used to say.

Mum's health didn't get any better and on occasions she was admitted to hospital. There were several hospital calls warning us to expect the worst. The last time was probably no different.

It was the middle of the night when Paul phoned me. We got ready to go to the hospital, but they rang again just before we left to say she had died.

When we arrived at Leighton Hospital, she looked at peace when we saw her. They had moved her from the ward into a private room. There was a vase of flowers on the table at the side which didn't look familiar. We sat there in silence for a while and then curiosity got the better and I went to look to see if there was a card on the flowers. There wasn't. I'm sure they weren't hers.

The things that run through your mind. My last conversation recalled, a raising of my voice. The places I hadn't taken her, the things promised which hadn't been done. Funny what comes back to haunt you afterwards. The things you shouldn't have said and, perhaps more importantly, the things you should have.

25

So, it's a spring evening and we're gathered in the front room of Paul's bungalow. I can't remember the exact date, but it wasn't long before Mum died. There's me and Mike, and Paul and his partner.

My mother is sitting in her chair by the fire, her checkered blanket over her knees as it invariably is, come rain or shine. She looks around us all and smiles. 'All here tonight, except David,' she says.

The television is on and we're not paying much attention.

'You see,' she says, looking around the four of us and smiling proudly. 'I did end up with all my boys, after all.'

26

So, they're all here somewhere, these shadowy relatives from the past, in the cemetery where I will be the first in four generations not to be interred.

The triple grave with Mum, Dad and Alice is over to the left. The headstone proclaiming:
"In loving memory of a dear husband and father
Frederick Roy Savill (no mention of the Goddard)
Died 10th Oct 1977
Aged 73
Also, a dear wife and mother
Joyce Winifred Savill
Died 25th Sept 1990
Aged 81
Together again."

A slight irony in retrospect, perhaps, with Gran Savill being in there as well.

The headstone has dipped at one end now, and the whole plot in front is a little uneven and sunken, almost as if there has been underground disturbance! It's not the only grave like that though, so, it must be subsidence, surely?

My sister-in-law, Joy, lies in a grave a little over to the right. David will go in that plot one day. Paul has reserved the one next to it. He said there was room in it for me, but I told him, 'No, you're alright.'

Over on the right are the graves of Gran and Grandad.
"Lizzie Ethel
died October 30th, 1968, aged 85.
John William Ralphs,
died November 24th, 1974, aged 90."

Next to them is a grander looking headstone for my Great Grandparents. You can just about make out the writing in the crumbling stone.

"Joseph Edwards
of Sandy Lane
died October 21st, 1918, aged 73.
Eliza
died 23rd February 1927, aged 82."

If you look between the headstones on the graves of my Grandparents and Great Grandparents, you can see a new memorial erected on the slope leading down towards the bottom of the cemetery.

It marks parish burials which were hitherto unrecognised. A list of sixty odd names written on it, looking a bit like a war memorial, a well-tended war memorial with flowers planted around it in the summer.

There, at the top of one of the columns of names is Philip Goddard Savill (spelt wrongly, they have added an 'e'). "Aged 2 months, buried in Grave 352. Date of death 12/5/1936."

There's a plaque on the front.

"Memorial to unmarked graves between the years 1876 and 1961. Many were buried as paupers with the fees being met by the Parish. The graves were discovered in 2003, the ground beneath them made good. The names of these forgotten persons are inscribed hereon in lasting memory of all such men, women and children."

Always sends a chill, every time I read it. Not all forgotten.

There is no reference to baby John. We did try to find out why he hadn't been mentioned along with all the others, but were told there was no record of him being buried there.

It has always been a story told within our family though, even if I was late to hear of it. Perhaps it was because he was buried without being christened or, perhaps it was just only ever one of those family stories? We'll never know for sure now.

I like to think he is there though, somewhere in that cemetery, in what remains of his pink fluffy woollen blanket.

27

So, I'm walking through the archway by the cemetery lodge. At one time there was a hand-written note by the outside water tap. It warned relatives that any flowers left on graves were likely to be eaten by rabbits. "They especially like chrysanthemums," it said.

Ahead of me are rows of headstones. They all seem familiar somehow; names from my childhood, conjuring up images of people I'd forgotten I knew, frozen in my mind's eye as children in their short trousers, baggy socks, and pinafore dresses.

Paul calls me away and breaks my chain of thought, leading me towards a group of people who are gathering around a grave, away to the left, their outlines silhouetted against the skyline in the fading afternoon light.

A coffin is waiting to be lowered into the freshly dug earth. We're at the funeral of a brother of a second cousin which my brother said we ought to attend.

Suddenly he calls out, far too loudly in the circumstances, 'Over there. Look. Quick!'

Some of the figures seem to hear and turn towards us and we both look guiltily away. After a moment, I chance a sideways glance towards the gaggle of darkly clad mourners.

'The grey-haired chap on the extreme right,' says Paul, in as loud a stage whisper as you're likely to hear.

I turn to look, getting another admonishment in the process. 'Not now! He'll see you.'

Tying a shoelace which doesn't need tying, I chance another glance. 'Yes?'

Paul smiles smugly. 'That's your other half-brother.'

THE END?

Yes, I think so. Seems appropriate to end it there, at the cemetery which holds so many memories.

My intention was simply to put down on paper the stories told me by my brothers and parents, together with my own recollections. The scant facts somehow add to the intrigue of the whole thing, raising more questions than answers. Versions of the same events turned out to be different depending on who you asked.

To this day I don't know if my half-brothers know who their father was and, if not, well, who am I to tell them now?

www.ingramcontent.com/pod-product-compliance
Lightning Source LLC
Chambersburg PA
CBHW050204130526
44591CB00034B/2111